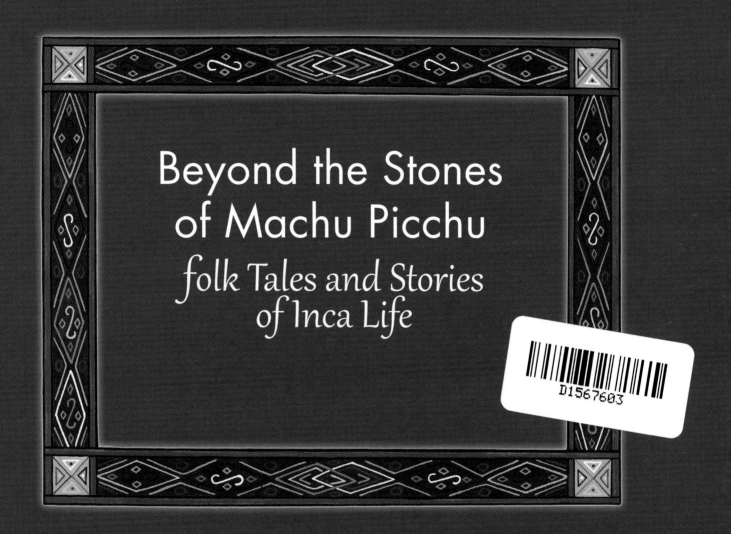

Beyond the Stones
of Machu Picchu

folk Tales and Stories
of Inca Life

Birthday
Gift
from
Pont?

2020

Beyond the Stones
of Machu Picchu

folk Tales and Stories
of Inca Life

BY

Elizabeth Conrad VanBuskirk

PAINTINGS BY

Angel L Callañaupa Alvarez

THRUMS

Publisher: Linda Ligon
Editor: Trish Faubion
Designer: Ann W. Douden

THRUMS Thrums LLC
306 North Washington
Loveland, Colorado USA

 Centro de Textiles Traditionales del Cusco
03 Avenida del Sol
Cusco, Peru

Printed and bound in China through Asia Pacific Offset

Library of Congress Control Number: 2013944307.
Cataloging-in-Publication (CIP) data applied for.

ISBN-13: 978-0-9838860-5-1

Dedication

I dedicate this book with love to my husband David VanBuskirk. He is not only my first reader, but has spent generous amounts of time helping me select and send out scans of Angel's paintings to our publisher for her review. He has provided his own fine photographs for me to use in all my lectures and school presentations. He is an enthusiastic collaborator in our Andean travels and pursuits, especially The Center for Traditional Textiles of Cusco. —e.v.b.

Welcome to the Andes

Would you like to fly like a condor? Do you ever wish you could talk with animals? When you visit extraordinary ruins, do you long to look past the great stones to truly, deeply feel the human history of a place and the ongoing life connections? If so, the nine stories in this book were written for you. They grew out of my own love for the people, the landscape, and the history of the region's great civilizations.

I am a writer, weaver, and teacher. Decades ago, looking for new ideas for my art and writing, I began to learn about traditional Andean weaving. I soon realized that the weaver's art could never be separated from the larger culture of the Incas and their predecessors. Their weavings are not merely functional and decorative, but carry forward values and traditions of a fascinating and significant past. Though treasured as family wealth, intricate textiles are sometimes considered to be a living presence in the household. The weavings tell stories about every aspect of Andean life. Inca villagers feel part of the land, cherishing rivers, mountains, rocks, caves, and outcroppings, and their intricate weaving is a major way they express the vital connection.

As I studied, and then began to visit again and again over the years, I learned that farmers, herders, and weavers maintain an intimate relationship with the soil, their animals, the forces of nature, and the spirits of the gods. Inca people today still hold ceremonies of appreciation. To *Pacha Mama*, Mother Earth, they present a woven cloth containing cookies, corn kernels, shells, small fertility figures, and other symbolic objects. People speak directly and familiarly to the great mountains, which in their Quechua language are called *Apus*. They regard the mountains not only as geographic features, but also as living entities, sacred fathers and mothers from whose great heights the rain flows to provide for all things living below.

Today's many millions of Quechua-speaking people of Peru are the spiritual heirs and true descendants of Inca civilization. The many who live in the small highland villages of the mountains still practice vital patterns and rituals that date back thousands of years. In these stories, which are based on both traditional folk tales and my own understanding of Andean culture, I want to share with you what I have learned. If we can even glimpse the lives and accomplishments of Inca people living today, we may reach a wider understanding and opportunity to ponder the hidden meanings that lie within and beyond the stones of Machu Picchu.

Beyond the Stones of Machu Picchu is for readers of all ages, especially travelers and would-be travelers who are drawn to Inca life, culture, art, and weaving. The book may also provide an opportunity for families to read aloud together. I particularly hope that Inca tales and stories will intrigue and open up a unique new world for young people.

Acknowledgments

Many people have shared in the development of this book about the distinctive Inca culture, land, and people. I first met Nilda Callañaupa Alvarez in 1982, and from then on she shared great amounts of information about her life and weaving, introduced me to other weavers, and helped me to learn Inca folk tales, some of which appear in this book. For her friendship and sharing, I am most grateful. I especially thank Angel Callañaupa Alvarez, whom I commissioned to paint illustrations for my own stories and who created paintings for the folk tales that I have here retold. Our happy collaboration comes to fruition in this book.

I want to express highest thanks to writers Kathleen McKinley Harris, Katherine Quimby Johnson, Sara Marshall, Nancy Means Wright, Laurel Neme, and Paula Diaco—members of my fiction writing group who have greatly supported my efforts, each in her own way, with critiques and edits, encouragement and enlightening discussions. I have learned much from them.

Special thanks to my mentors in writing, David Weinstock and Sally R. Brady, to the late historian Frances Richardson Keller, and to archaeologist-art historian of Mesoamerica and Peru, Clemency Coggins, with whom I studied at The Radcliffe Institute. I celebrate the life and work of the late Ed Franquemont, who shared with my husband and me his wide knowledge, theoretical ideas, and love of Inca people and weaving. Thanks go to Nancy Silberg for helping me to grow.

Thank you to anthropologist Serena VanBuskirk, sole reader of the whole almost-finished book who, with enthusiasm, helped me sort out the overall themes. My appreciation to my brother David Conrad for opening many opportunites to disseminate knowledge about the Inca culture, especially in the courses we taught together at the University of Vermont. David generously read each story to point out any discrepancies and make suggestions about the use of language in discussing other cultures. Thank you, Ann Porter and Chris Fearon of the Robert Hull Fleming Museum of the University of Vermont. Thank you Debbie Bushey for scanning, organizing, and carefully preserving Angel's art works.

I appreciate the work and publications of the late anthropologist, Robert Randall, whose writings about the Inca *Qoyllu Riti* ceremony helped me understand this Inca ritual pilgrimage. An interview with Jose Flores also provided valuable background. Thanks also to anthropologist Gary Urton for his work and illuminating books about Inca culture.

Thank you, Linda Ligon, our publisher, founder of Interweave Press and of the new and growing multicultural imprint, Thrums Books.

This book was made possible, in part, by a Barbara Karlin Grant from the Society of Children's Book Writers and Illustrators. — e.v.b.

Contents

Inca Folk Tales Retold

Folk tales are retold in every generation, especially in societies without written language. In the retelling, the tales change, and this is a good thing. Change and adaptation ensure that new listeners can understand the stories, take them into their hearts, and pass them along in turn. In effect, learning the tales lets us become privy to strange and encoded aspects of life. I hope you will read, enjoy, and then retell these stories in your own way.

These first glimpses into Inca life are based directly on tales Angel Callañaupa heard from his grandmother. Angel told many of these tales to me in Spanish, and his sister Nilda Callañaupa Alvarez translated his short versions into English. I have chosen three of Angel's tales and expanded upon each, adding the background needed for me to understand them. And now I give them to you.

Alight now in the Andes.

THE
Gift of Quinoa

Once there lived a lively and clever—but very mean—fox. Nothing bothered Fox. In times of drought or disaster, he closed his ears to the stories of others' troubles. He walked like a great and mighty gentleman and wore beautiful weavings that he had stolen from terrified young llama herders while at the same time devouring their lunches.

All the animals on the mountainside feared Fox. But one day, all their ears twitched with curiosity when Fox's voice drifted in the clear Andean air.

"Listen to me, dear friends. This very night, Father Mountain will hold a banquet at his palace in the sky. This news comes straight from Condor."

Everyone knew that Fox and Condor were friends. Condor was the messenger of the Great *Apu*, Father Mountain, the powerful mountain spirit who watched over all creatures on the mountainside. How could they doubt the news? Duck, Mother Guinea Pig, and Rabbit crept close to Fox. Without warning, Fox grabbed Duck's neck.

"I need you, Duck," he said, "I cannot reach the palace without wings." Duck tried to flap free but could not. Mother Guinea Pig raced to help, a long stub of cactus in her paw. She thrust the spikes into Fox, who leapt so high that Duck easily escaped. But Fox did a double twirl and reached for Mother Guinea Pig.

"You fool, I need you too. I will start a little fire and roast you right now—just in case we have a prominent visitor."

Rabbit saw that the log on which Fox stood was unbalanced and teetered slightly. He put a stone under one side and jumped hard on the log. Into the air Fox flew, letting go of Mother Guinea Pig. Fox, the great entertainer, landed in a nearby pond.

As Fox yelled insults, jumped, and splashed, who should appear high in the sky but Condor. Fox was out of the water in no time, shaking until he came out almost dry. He raced to the spot where Condor would likely land and lay his beautiful weaving on a stone.

"Welcome, Friend Condor, King of the Birds," he said. "Here is a pedestal just for you. Do perch. And if you are hungry, I can, with little trouble, offer you a delicious meal."

"We will talk later," Condor said. "First I have come to present invitations to the other animals."

Condor gestured to Parrot, who flew low and lifted his wings. Bright flower petals floated down. Condor spoke, "Dear animals, please help yourselves. Take back two invitations for each family."

Brimming with excitement, the animals divided the invitations. After they ran off, Condor said, "Alas, Fox, I must deliver bad news to you. You are not to be invited. Father Mountain does not like certain events he has seen lately. He believes that you are likely to disrespect his rules and his palace and that you might bully other guests. Worst of all, he sees you as a greedy soul. He fears you might take something of great significance that is not yours."

"Condor," Fox said, "Father Mountain lives high in the sky. He has not learned to trust me yet because he does not understand some things. My role is to entertain. All creatures love my creative play. Even when I tease, they are intrigued and want more. But at the Castle in the Sky, I will stand out as an easy guest, even subdued if you wish. I would never cause any kind of disturbance."

Fox treated Condor to a remarkable display of jumps and twists. Up and down the slopes he flung himself, ending with a dozen cartwheels.

Fox bowed. "Take me with you, Condor. You will forever be proud of your faithful friend."

"You are hard to resist, Fox. You have always been a faithful, joyous friend. I cannot leave you. I know Father Mountain will understand."

Fox climbed onto Condor's back, and they flew high enough to soar over the gleaming glaciers near the mountain's top. Finally, through a high mist, appeared the outlines of the Great Castle in the Sky. It was made of ice and inlaid with bright jewels and golden disks. Suddenly the Great *Apu*, Father Mountain, appeared on a cloud. He was not happy to see Fox, but he listened to Condor, his trusted messenger.

Father Mountain welcomed the other guests as they arrived on the backs of their winged friends. When everyone was seated in the great hall, he called for a moment of silence and thanksgiving. All eyes closed. In front of Fox lay a golden plate piled with fine food. Hastily he pressed the plate to his face, gobbled every morsel, and licked the plate clean.

"Dear Friends," Father Mountain announced, "Even from high up here, I look down on the hard times below when crops fail and everyone suffers from hunger. Today, I present to all creatures of the earth a unique new grain, called quinoa. This grain grows as fast as magic. The sprouts are powerful and can survive on high slopes and in extreme weather. I have seen quinoa plants spread as far as any of you can see and grow in the rich colors of humans' woven *mantas*."

As Father Mountain reached down, Fox grabbed the gigantic sack of quinoa and dumped the entire bag of seeds over his head and body. The seeds sank into his thick fur. He stepped on a stool, took a regal stance, raised a paw, and laughed.

Father Mountain, who had never seen such a performance, stepped back in stunned silence. The great hall filled with furious conversations. What would the *Apu* do to stop Fox?

All eyes were on Fox as he grabbed Duck's food, gulped down all the delicacies, and cracked the golden plate over Duck's head.

"Fox," Father Mountain ordered. "Leave my Palace, at once!"

"That is not possible, dear *Apu*, for I have no wings."

"Wings or not, the wind will now remove you from this sacred place." A gust of wind moved toward Fox.

"Save me, Condor," Fox cried, "or you will forever lose your best friend." Tears ran down the Fox's furry face and a few seeds, even so slightly watered, began to sprout.

"See what you have done!" Condor replied." Who can help you now?" But, being a bird of action, Condor quickly braided a long thick rope, wound it around Fox and led his former friend out of the Palace. "I will hold this end here, if I can, and you too hold tight," he said just as a strong wind pushed Fox off the edge of the cloud.

The Gift of Quinoa

"Here I go, lucky ones below," Fox called, dangling from the rope, twisting and floating in the air. But Fox was soon perturbed by an intruder.

"Parrot, what are you doing high in my space? Fly somewhere else. I cannot be near a nasty bird like you."

"Do not speak to me like that," said Parrot. "I could bite that dangling rope."

"How would a coward like you find such nerve? I am protected by mighty forces above." Fox merrily jerked the line to add a little drama.

"Just watch this, Fox!" Parrot took one quick snap at the rope.

"Look what you have done," Fox screamed. "You have cut my life line. I am loose in the air!"

Fox soon lost sight of Parrot. As he fell, he gained great speed. The sky, mountains, and clouds slid by and the earth rose toward him. On the slope below, scared little guinea pigs ran in all directions.

"Dear Guinea Pigs," he called. "Look what they have done to me now! If I hit the earth, it will be no joke. Bring weavings and lay them below to soften my fall."

But the little ones threw cactus stubs instead.

"Help," cried Fox. The guinea pigs raced away.

Down crashed Fox onto the sharp spiky pile. He landed with a hard thud and sank deep into Mother Earth. Some who saw Fox fall say that his head landed last, and a smirk, then a wink, were his last expressions.

The quinoa seeds that flew out of his fur suddenly began to sprout. With great speed they grew tall. In no time the hillside was covered with bright quinoa plants—magenta, rose, and orange stalks, some tipped with contrasting darker shades.

As the years went by, thanks to the *Apu* and the accidental planting by Fox, protein-rich quinoa became a staple crop to feed those who live in the Andes Mountains of South America.

The Gift of Quinoa

THE
Bear Prince

Once there was an Inca girl named Kanta who lived with her parents in a stone house that clung high on the western side of the mountain. Every day, when she herded the family llamas, Kanta walked along a ridge where she could look down the steep slope to the eastern cloud forest that led to the jungle far out of sight.

Each morning, before Kanta left home with the llamas, her mother warned her, "Always stay on our side of the mountain, Kanta. Take care or you could find yourself on a path that leads down the other side, to the jungle." Her father often spoke of the jungle, inhabited by wild creatures, where the trees were so close and the leaves so enormous they could completely surround a person. He too warned her, "Be careful."

Every day, Kanta found different flat spaces for her llamas to graze. As they grazed, she sat on rocks that sometimes felt so smooth and warm she wondered if they had once been live people. She had heard stories of girls who disobeyed their parents and were turned to stone. Sometimes her mind wandered to the days of her great Inca ancestors. She imagined that the emperor himself might have passed this way.

Kanta also liked to think about the mountain's "other side." She sat near the edge of a drop-off where the clouds rose from the depths. She could touch and taste the clouds. This closeness to the distant views and moving mist made her happy.

Kanta loved to weave and as she watched her llamas she sang. One day a great Andean bear, drawn to the sound of her sweet voice, sat nearby and accompanied her with his flute. Their music soared like the flight of a condor.

When Kanta dared to glance up, the bear appeared as a handsome Inca prince with beautiful black hair. He was larger and more powerful than any man she had ever met. Kanta was overcome. Her hands forgot how to weave. She let several balls of yarn roll downhill until they caught in the bushes.

Every day he came, her prince brought her sweet fruits that she had never tasted. At home she ate only potatoes, quinoa, carrots, and other foods that could grow high in the mountains. Now she tasted passion fruits, the sweet pulp of bananas, and huge hunks of sweet melon.

Kanta lived in dizzy confusion. When the clouds swirled up from the other side of the mountain, they seemed to hold her in a deep hug that would never end. On a clear day, when she looked down on the network of winding paths, her body felt limp and she hastened to move away from the edge.

When her prince was nearby, Kanta dreamed of him chasing back the ghosts that might come out of caves, of him catching her if she should fall, and of him someday taking her to the jungle so she could glimpse the wonders of which her father had spoken so often. When she went home at night, she kept her thoughts to herself.

The cold season began, and Kanta shivered when she stood in the wind. Finally her prince came close and hugged her gently. She flushed with warmth and reached up to touch his long black hair that seemed as glossy as her own.

After that, Kanta looked forward to their daily embraces. One crisp cold morning her prince hugged her tightly and spoke words she could hardly believe, "I have a very nice house in the jungle where the sweet fruits grow. Come with me, and I will protect you and bring you whatever you please. Where I live we do not have to work hard, like your family in the mountains. And you will have a safe and comfortable place to sleep."

Enchanted by the ministrations of her prince, Kanta forgot her llamas. She forgot her family and her village. He begged her to follow him on one of the winding paths that made

25

The Bear Prince

her curious. By the side of her new love, she felt brave and excited.

The journey was longer and more difficult than Kanta expected. Often she and her family had walked or run through the mountains for hours and days to visit distant godparents or relatives. But today, as she raced to keep up, her sandals took flight over small stones that rolled her down-slope repeatedly. She struggled to steady herself until she heard a deep voice from the path far below.

"Climb on my back. It will be easier for you." She threw her arms around the wide neck of her gallant prince and hugged him tightly. At first Kanta recalled the rhythms of her early childhood when she rode in a *manta* on her mother's back. But this sensation did not last. They swerved so fast she could hardly hold on.

"How long?" she asked.

"Just around the bend, my love." The prince plunged into a turbulent river and splashed across, the water almost pulling Kanta in. Her hat fell off but her prince splashed deeper to scoop it up for her.

"How much longer?" she asked again, as it grew hotter. They pushed through thick growth. Leaves and branches slapped back against Kanta's bare legs. For the first time, she thought of her father's warnings and of her family, high on the mountain.

In the middle of the second night, in a small clearing surrounded by thick bushes and hanging vines, they stopped so suddenly that Kanta slid off. In dim light, Kanta saw no prince, but a great Andean bear standing by her side.

"Who are you? Where are we?" she demanded. He glanced at a cave high above them.

"You are not the prince I knew in the mountains," she declared. "And this is no fine place to live." She cried and scolded and blamed the bear until he carried her into the cool cave, wrapped her in a soft animal skin, and lay close to keep her warm. Weary, she fell asleep.

The morning sun rose, but Kanta lay in near darkness. In her stupor, she mumbled, "In this cave, what can we eat?"

"No need to worry," said her bear. "We are in the jungle where there is always food."

Off he went and returned with more food than she had ever imagined. Bananas, pineapples, mangos, avocados, even large-kernelled treats of corn. But Kanta had no appetite, even for the most delicious offerings. Shocked and tearful, she

could only think about her family. They would have been alarmed when the llamas came home without her. Every villager must have spread out in the mountains and be looking for her.

As time passed, Kanta tried to accept her life with the bear, but she was too unhappy even to weave. Only at night, when her warm companion held her and she felt the pleasure of his love, did she find solace.

One day, Kanta realized she was to have a baby. This brought her back to life in a

The Bear Prince

new way. She spent hours every day weaving a beautiful *manta* for carrying the child. How she desired to hold a little one in her arms!

Kanta's time came, and her bear did all he could to help. When she first saw the baby boy, Kanta wept and wailed, "No!" for he was human only from the waist up. From the waist down, he had the body of a bear.

Their little boy was healthy and easy to please. In no time Kanta delighted to his soft gurgles, his smiles, and his wide-open eyes. She grew to love the little boy with all her heart. When he was old enough, and not playing with his father, she spent hours telling him stories about her past life in a distant place.

When she thought the boy could understand, Kanta explained to him, "I'm so unhappy away from my true home. I have longed for my family and people since I came to live here. Now I must find my way back. But Father Bear says that I must not go—for I will never return."

The little boy loved his mother, and the sadness on her face alarmed him. He would go to take care of her on her trip, he declared. But what could he do to help her start the journey? Kanta told him of a plan.

In no time she heard the child ask, "Papa, will you go find me what I have always wanted—a black llama?" A black llama is a rare creature. It would take great effort to bring back such a prize. But his father answered, "For you, my son, I

will find you what you want." The bear collected food for his family and soon set off on his quest.

Only then did Kanta hesitate. She was sad to leave their home and her dear bear who cared so well for them all. But she was excited about the journey. Mother and son plunged into the high vegetation. They tunneled under low bushes and leaves, winding their way upward on the stony path. They walked across small valleys, forded streams and rivers, and struggled over giant boulders. Finally, at journey's end, they passed a great waterfall and walked hand in hand until they climbed onto the high ridge where Kanta once herded her beloved llamas.

Kanta was happy to see her son's excitement. For the first time he could look up at the endless blue sky. He stared into the far distance. He pointed out the soft but lively mist that floated between layers of mountains.

Kanta's parents were overjoyed to see their daughter. Her mother stroked Kanta's long black hair. But both parents were dismayed when she told them how she had run off with a bear and lived in a cave in the jungle. At first they drew back in alarm when she presented their strange grandson, half human, half bear.

However, it was hard not to love the surprise grandson —his delight in their meeting, his easy friendliness, his evident love for his mother. Kanta's parents determined to make him part of the family. As a benefit, they pointed out, he could help with the heavy everyday tasks.

The Bear Prince

But the boy declared, "Don't forget my father. He is very strong and has gone to find me a black llama. Soon he will find Mama and me and take us back." Kanta's parents waited until they were alone to express their fears.

"This bear will arrive any time now. We must stop him. We can't wait." Together they formed a plan. They poured boiling water in a giant pot and covered the pot with a large and lovely

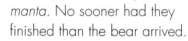

manta. No sooner had they finished than the bear arrived.

Kanta's parents received the bear heartily. They told him that their daughter and grandson would soon return. As is the custom in greeting a guest, Kanta's mother said, "Come in and sit on my favorite *manta*."

The bear, happy to be so accepted, sat back on the lovely cloth. Immediately he sank. Steam engulfed him. His deep howl of pain shook the walls as he struggled to pull himself up. But the pot's sides were straight and too slick for his paws to grasp. "Help!" was the great bear's final howl. Kanta's parents were happy to think that they had saved their daughter.

From far away Kanta and the boy heard the bear's howls and hastened to the house.

"Look what you have done," Kanta cried. "Although I deceived my bear husband, he was kind and thoughtful and always treated us well. Only now do I see how much I loved him."

The son cried, "Papa, let me help you out." He struggled to save his father but it was too late.

Kanta would not speak to her parents. She went off to weave alone, or she and her son together took the animals to graze. She recognized the depth of her son's grief, and she constantly feared that his father's spirit would draw him back to his original home.

As her son grew up, he began to look more and more human, but everyone marveled at his strength. He could pull up trees by their roots. He could carry enormous stones. His mother named him Pablucha, "Bear Son." He soon made her proud. He was invited to perform a bear dance at every fiesta held in the village.

One day, Kanta stood outside the door, spinning. Along came her beloved Pablucha, wearing his white fiesta mask, racing downhill. He passed her without stopping, and as he ran, his body gradually turned into that of a full bear. Kanta called out, but without looking back, Pablucha disappeared from sight. Kanta stood by the door, pulling her hair into a tight braid. "Now I must forever live my life without the two that I love."

Since that time, Inca fiestas have featured a great bear, Pablucha, or his bear father, Ukuku. At fiestas the people play the bear role to endow themselves with powerful abilities. Pablucha is thought sometimes to change into a man or a boy, but never for long. It is also rumored that he must always return home by way of a winding path on the other side of the mountain.

The Bear Prince

To Live Like Humans!

Kuri Inti, his wife, and three mouse children lived a life of misery and fear in a farmer's house overseen by Big Boss Cat. Cat laughed when he made them push the grinding stone in the granary room. He was happy each day to see all five fall down with exhaustion, five little limp bodies.

Cat invented games. With exaggerated stealth he pretended to block every cheese route. Sometimes he dangled the cheese over their heads until they risked getting too close. Both mice parents prickled with fear that Cat might suddenly pounce, and a precious mouse life would end as a heap of bones.

Kuri Inti told his children, "Some day soon, our family will escape this miserable existence."

"We can survive on our own," said Mama.

"We will live like humans!" Papa promised.

"When, Papa, when?" Day and night the children thought about living like humans. Would they wear clothes like humans and dance at fiestas?

Late one night Papa hid in the courtyard and whispered words that reached sleepy Cat's ear. "Oh Cat, we are likely to run away one of these days. Won't you be surprised? And we will start living like humans."

Cat, who was almost asleep, sprang awake. "Little fools, you would not know what to do on your own. You would be right back."

"You will be very surprised," said Kuri Inti. "My fine wife and I are both well educated. We have studied how humans live. We have observed every human activity."

"Ha, you are a funny little fellow. But I need my sleep. If you wake me again, I will push the foot plow off the wall and hope it lands on you."

Kuri Inti ran back to his family who had been listening behind the wall. "Get ready to fly away," he said. "We will escape this very night!"

The mouse family scampered out of the human's house, leaving the nooks and crevices and tunnels that had sheltered them all their lives. All three little ones trembled with fear, but they ran as fast as they could until they were far away. At a field of stone outcroppings, the children stopped to play until Papa commanded, "Keep on the move. We must be stalwart and strong. We are the first mice family who will live like humans."

Kuri Inti would have continued his words of vision and glory, for he was given to bouts of enthusiasm, but out popped Viscacha, Rabbit's southern cousin. "Such shocking words, Mouse! Here in the mountains it is too high and cold for trees, let alone little mice. Even humans have to be exceedingly clever to survive. Trying to live here, on your own, you will meet terrible storms that can blow you to the nests of condors."

The children pressed against Mama and hid their tails. "Don't worry," Papa said. "We have the whole day ahead to find a perfect place to settle for our first night."

The whole day turned out to be quite an unexpected test of mouse will. A fierce wind blew so hard that all three young ones struggled just to avoid being blown back. They kept their bodies close to the earth and tried to hang on to either Mama or Papa.

The wind stopped, but dark clouds grew together above them like a soaked and sagging ceiling cloth. Enough rain came down to bring a dry arroyo alive and roaring nearby. They heard the terrible noise of rushing water, but, by following Papa's clever zigs and zags, they all escaped the rising torrent.

The rain stopped. The sun turned the world yellow.

To Live Like Humans

Quickly the mice's soggy fur dried. But in no time, they were surrounded by ferocious heat with no comforting shade in sight. Little mice feet could no longer run on the red dirt, pebbles, and stones. Everything they touched felt like coals in a fire.

"We might as well go back to Cat!" the smallest mouse cried.

"Be patient," Papa said as he set off and returned with two mouse-sized leaves. "Maybe you can rest in a bit of leaf shade. Later we will find our perfect patch of land to start life again. We will live as happily as humans."

They heard a squawk, and Parrot landed nearby. "Like humans? What do I hear? You are so small. Skimpy leaves are no cover for any family. Señor Mouse, what needs to happen to bring you some sense?"

The smallest mouse popped out from under his leaf. "I will eat you up, Parrot," he squeaked and pulled the leaf around his little body.

The oldest mouse child squeaked, "Beware. Our Papa is Señor Kuri Inti, named for the power of the sun."

Papa said, "See here. These are brave children. They will never give up."

To everyone's relief, Parrot fluttered her wings and flew away.

Mama said, "Let's stay here until the sun goes down, and then we can huddle together in the nice cool mountain air and enjoy happy dreams."

The sun moved over the tips of the mountain peaks. As darkness fell, so did the Andean mountain chill that went straight through the bones of each small body. Their little teeth felt like chattering icicles. "Papa, Mama," they cried. "It is too cold. Parrot was right. Tonight we are going to freeze." Finally, two children cuddled against Mama, and the oldest against Papa who sat up all night, half alert, half asleep.

When morning came, Mama and Papa made a fire. The children hugged themselves to keep warm, but they were glad that the sun still hid behind rising clouds.

"Everyone listen!" said Mama. "We are all hungry, and to live like humans, we must now find food and cook. Back at the house, I watched the farmer's wife cook all the family's food. Often she had to take great pots of stew to those working in the fields. I need you to find me a few kernels of corn, some potatoes, and beans. Then I will cook you all a splendid human soup."

To their surprise, Guinea Pig poked up her furry face. "What is this, Mama Mouse? You cook a human soup?"

"We are living like human beings," said the smallest mouse.

"Who allows such talk? You mice are too small and insignificant to find food out here on your own. Your family will starve. We guinea pigs know that our place is on the floor of human kitchens. Every day the family tosses us leafy leftovers. So we eat well—until they are ready to eat us, of course. There is no way to avoid that untimely end. But we live as we are meant to. Every creature has a place, and you too must know yours."

"Never!" said the oldest little mouse. "Never," said the middle mouse. "We won't," said the smallest mouse.

"Don't live a life of dreams," said Guinea Pig, and off she ran.

To Live Like Humans

Papa's pride sent him whirling. He skip-hopped over rocks. He squeaked, "You children are learning how to live. Now let's go fetch Mama what she needs."

Soon they had collected several old cobs of corn, a few potatoes, and beans. Under a bush, the middle child even found three clay pots to roll back to Mama.

Mama's stew was delicious. The children licked their lips and wiped their little mouths on their fur.

At the end of the day the family traveled down the slope to where the smell of eucalyptus trees kept their noses busy sniffing. Nearby they discovered some curious caves. A friendly looking mouse popped out of one, and Mama explained, "We have endured wind, rain, sun, and terrible cold. Can we find shelter here?"

The mouse welcomed them. The family cuddled in the comforting darkness, and by morning all were rested and ready for a grand new endeavor.

Mama asked, "To live like human beings, what shall we do next?"

Everyone offered suggestions.

"We need a blanket to make us warm at night," said the middle mouse, "and clothes for when it is cold or rainy."

"Something to keep us off the cold ground," said the littlest mouse.

The oldest child said, "A good carrying cloth. We need to bring back loads of food for Mama to cook."

"You are describing humans' woven *mantas*!" Mama exclaimed. "I hope we can learn to weave."

"Weavings would make us as proud as humans!" said Papa.

The parents let the three little ones run off to find bits of fluff that hung on bushes. They plucked here and there until they heard voices and saw two human girls walking up the hill, carrying large clay jugs. One girl said, "Look at those tiny mice. They are collecting bits of fur that our llamas rubbed off on the prickly bushes. How clever they are."

The girl bent down. "What are you doing, little ones?"

"We are going to make yarn," said the oldest.

The youngest could not resist the opportunity to enlighten their new acquaintance. "We are going to live like humans."

There was a long pause while the three mice waited for the usual words of warning. But the girl laughed. "Good for you, mousies. But if you really want to make yarn, you will need to use drop spindles."

The mice looked sad.

"Maybe I can help," the girl said. "My brother makes tiny chairs and tables from bottle caps. Maybe he could make a tiny wood spindle for each of you." She picked up her water jug. "Come back tomorrow," she called back as she continued up the hill.

When Mama heard the news, she danced a toe-to-nose routine. "Drop spindles! I have watched humans. They can spin such fine yarn by turning their spindles. When they walk, they always spin. Maybe soon we will be making yarn for our weaving."

The next day the three mouse children returned to the hillside. The human girl finally appeared, soaked with water, and carrying her pot. "I didn't forget you," she said, "but we were playing at the well, singing and dancing. We dumped

To Live Like Humans

water on each other. We had such fun." Out of her hat she pulled four tiny spindles. "These are for you, and one extra."

Four spindles! The little mice did their best to entertain their new friend. They tried new tricks with their tails and squeaked songs of joy.

The girl said, "If you clever little mice learn to weave, I would like to see that."

Mama was so happy that she wanted to try to spin right away. Soon all the mice learned to twist their scruffy fluffs into yarn.

Before long they asked Mama, "Where do humans find colored yarn?"

"You have a real treat ahead," said Mama.

They all followed her along the hillsides, snipping off and dragging back quantities of bright yellow *kiko* flowers.

With Papa's help they heated water in a pot. After they pushed in the heaps of yellow flowers, steam rose around the flowers, and the hot water turned bright yellow. They had fun dropping in their batches of yarn.

The next day the whole family ran deep into the valley to collect cochineal, little bugs that grow between the thorns on prickly cactus. Into the pot went the bugs. The water and yarn turned a lovely rose red. After that, the mice discovered they could dye yarn different colors by using leaves, flowers, and roots. There was much squeaky delight.

It was time to weave. Mama told them that humans make a new backstrap loom for each new weaving. In the end, the loom, with its sticks cut off and loops pulled out, becomes the weaving. "Watch and see," she said.

First Mama made a little loom for the oldest child. The other two complained, but Mama said they would be next.

Papa helped Mama wind the warp to make a miniature but real *manta* that would be too tiny for humans but an ample size for mice. While the children watched, Papa helped Mama count, measure, and wind their colored yarns around two tall sticks. Everyone felt proud to see the first part of a big weaving accomplished.

But Mama said bad words as she struggled to turn the many well-ordered colored strands of yarn into a loom. The two smallest mice squeaked, "Mama, we are ready now!"

"Leave me alone, all of you," Mama said.

The two youngest played all day while they waited for Mama's help to make a little loom of their own. The oldest tangled up a lot of yarn, trying to weave alone.

Finally Mama said, "I have done it. I have turned our warp of yarn into a big loom! Now I will help you." They all watched carefully and soon began their first narrow weavings. The youngest mouse worked so hard that he had to take a nap. But he woke up and tried again.

In no time, all three little ones made their first weavings. As with human children, weaving became a happy part of their lives, always accompanied by jokes and laughter. Mama worked on her loom. When her *manta* was done, everyone begged to try it on.

Soon Mama made Papa a magnificent red *poncho*. He stood up straight and spread out his front paws. "I feel as great as any human."

The oldest mouse said, "You look distinguished, Señor Papa Kuri Inti! But humans have fiestas where they dress up

To Live Like Humans

in their best *ponchos* and weavings and sing and dance
and play tricks and have fun. When can we do that?"

"Any time. As soon as we are ready," said Papa.

"That's what we want!" said the middle mouse child. Papa
picked him up and whirled him in the air. "My son, we will
have a fine fiesta. You already have a few mouse friends. Invite
them all, and we will invite every other mouse we have met."

Mama made weavings for all her children, and for a few
friends too. She sewed shirts and made Papa a vest.

The big fiesta day came with a bright blue sky but
enough clouds to keep all the mice cool. What excitement!

The soup was delicious and so was the *chicha* beer that Papa made from corn kernels.

"It is time to dance," Papa said, and what dancing and delight they all enjoyed.

Then someone dared ask, "Pardon, Señor Kuri Inti, you are living like humans, but you and your family dwell in a cave. Will you ever live in a house with a roof and walls of red earth or stone?"

"I have watched humans build many a house," said Papa, "and I know their secret. No one family builds a house alone. Everyone helps and works together. For example, I, Kuri Inti, need help. Who will help me to build our house? Then we will put together a house for every mouse here assembled."

There was a bit of grumbling, but the guests were in such good spirits that they softly squeaked to each other, "It sounds like hard work, for we are not great and strong like humans. But let's try—and hope the excellent Señor keeps his promise."

All the mice toasted Papa and immediately wanted to start their work. Some mice collected rocks. Some dug up clay to make red adobe bricks. Others dragged over the long posts that Papa had been collecting. The children ran off to cut *ichu* grass for the roof.

"In just a few nights we will be cozy in our own house," Papa told his family.

The oldest little mouse stayed to help. The other two ran to look for their human friend. They found her asleep in the sun, her jug by her side. Quiet as mice can be, they sat on her *manta* and set up their little looms to weave.

"We must finish our weavings quickly. How happy she will be to wake and find our little presents. She will know then that we have learned to weave."

"And that we are living like human beings," said the youngest mouse.

To Live Like Humans

When they finished and placed their presents of two lovely tiny weavings on the girl's *manta*, they went back to see Papa. Already there was what looked like a real human house, almost ready for them to move in.

That night, when Papa arrived back at the cave, he was almost too weary to talk. But he had news for Mama Mouse so they huddled in a corner of the cave. "When I stopped working on the house, the moon was so bright it made long shadows—and soon I saw that one was moving, slinking behind outcroppings and rocks and behind the one adobe wall we finished."

Mama leapt up on her hind legs. "What is he doing here?"

Papa Kuri Inti held his frightened wife. "By all means, don't fear what we don't know. He has probably come to see what we have done. After all we have survived so far, we can certainly handle a cat."

Mama lay back. She had to admit that her husband was right. "He should be too impressed to see what we mice have accomplished to want to eat us. Anyway our weavings would not taste good and imagine him trying to undress us!"

The smallest mouse came over to join the conversation. "Papa," he said, "the house is almost done. We are living like humans. Now we will have no more troubles in the world. Yippee."

"Where did you get such an idea?" Papa asked his son.

"We mice are brave and strong, and we work hard. Now we will have a happy life, without worries or hardships, just like humans."

"In the morning we will talk," Papa said. "It has been too busy a day. Let's all sleep soundly through the night."

To Live Like Humans

Stories of Inca Life

Each of the stories that follow describes a milestone or significant event in an Inca person's life and the first encounters, new experiences, and changes that form identity.

One early ritual for Inca young people involves caring for the family's llamas or sheep. Children, sometimes as young as six years old, encounter freedom, excitement, and danger as they care for the village's herds on high slopes far from home.

When Inca children are very young, learning to spin and learning to weave are significant events. The skills, independence, and creativity they develop are carried with them into adulthood. Traditionally, weavers made exquisite *mantas*, *ponchos*, bags, belts, and ritual items for celebration. The creations were intended for families to wear and use and to enhance the dignity of the family. Recently, however, village weavings provide a way to improve peoples' lives in many other ways. For example, weavers of Chinchero sold belts in Cusco to raise money to provide glass windows for their childrens' school. Even when the works are made to sell, weaving remains an act of love, solace, solidarity with others, and joy.

These stories might be called "original folk tales." The plots and characters are my own, but the stories are rooted in the culture I have studied for so long and which I want to represent faithfully. If I had been born into the Inca culture, these stories are the kind I would have wished my grandmothers to tell. In writing them, I had the added inspiration of Angel Callañaupa's paintings, which taught me more than words can say.

Beyond the Stones of Machu Picchu

THE
First Hair Cutting

It is a custom in the land of the Incas to honor and celebrate the milestones in a person's life. Each special life event provides a chance to add godparents as new relatives to the family. In the Andes, a godparent is a member of the family for life. By inviting friends and distant relatives to serve as compadres and comadres for children, a family can gather members who live on the highest mountain tops, in river valleys, the jungle, the city, even as far away as the coast. In the harsh Andean climate, family members from different regions can help in times of need.

It was the end of the season of rain. Plants grew and animals grew, and the celebration of Ana's First Hair Cutting would make her family grow. In the courtyard of her house, Ana sat on a stone bench while her mother brushed her long hair. Her mother's hands parted and twisted her hair into twenty-five slender braids, each braid tied with a *jakima*, a long woven ribbon.

"Ana, you are five now. This is a great day for you, the day of your first Hair Cutting. After today, your life will change in wonderful new ways because you will be a big girl with a big girl's hair growing every day." Ana was not so sure about "change." Already there had been many new things in her life. After her older sister, Fidelia, started school, Ana had been left home by herself. Then her *abuela* stopped helping her learn to spin yarn, and she felt more alone. Now she was sure that she would always be alone—no more time, even with her mother. Ana already hurt as much as a piglet caught in hail. How they scream! She could not scream but what *could* she do?

Ana's mother finished braiding Ana's hair and went to the kitchen to prepare food for the feast. Ana's brothers brought in wood for the fire. Musicians arrived, and her father opened the door to let them in. Everyone seemed excited about Ana's Hair Cutting—everyone except Ana. She picked up the puppy and climbed to the balcony. She stroked his soft ears. "Lucky puppy. No one cuts *your* fur."

Ana heard voices on the road outside. She ran down to open the door. It was *Tia* Lela from the valley. Ana loved to have *Tia* Lela visit, although today Ana knew that *Tia* Lela had come to be Godmother of Ana's First Hair Cutting.

Ana ran into *Tia* Lela's arms.

"Dear Ana, this is a big day for both of us."

"But *Tia*, what if I don't want my hair cut?"

"Ana, when I was your age, I felt that way too."

Tia Lela teased Ana. She pulled a braid, two braids, three braids. "These braids will bring our families together. Soon you will visit me in the valley. We will take long walks along the river and spin together. Would you like that?"

"I would, *Tia*. But what about my braids?"

"Wait and see. Good things are about to happen."

Delicious smells mixed with the morning mist above the tile roofs of Ana's village. One by one, her favorite people arrived. Everyone hugged Ana.

Ana's mother, aunts, and cousins brought out steaming pots of onion, lamb, and potato stew, plates of giant crispy fava beans, fresh bread, and—best of all—roasted corn with melted cheese. Everyone ate and drank, joked and laughed. Ana sat between *Tia* Lela and her sister, Fidelia. With longing Ana looked at Fidelia's long thick glossy braids.

Ana's father stood. "Welcome, dear family, dear friends. We thank you for coming to share Ana's First Hair Cutting."

The time had come, but Ana could hardly listen. She thought, "I can't give up my hair. Without my hair no one will know who I am. My hair is mine. I love my hair, better than my toes or my fingers, and even my ears."

Ana looked around at the twenty-five special people who were there, each to cut one of her braids. All of them had once had a First Hair Cutting that had made their families bigger by adding godparents. In this way, her family had relatives as

far as she could walk, even farther. Maybe it would be nice for Ana to bring *Tia* Lela's family into her own. Sitting next to *Tia*, she thought, "There *will* be good times ahead. Maybe it is worth giving up my hair."

Ana stood and put her arms around her father's neck. "Papa, when do we start?"

Papa hugged Ana. In the courtyard he gently lifted her onto the table. Everyone gathered around. Her father continued, "The ancestors watch as our family and Lela's unite to make both families large and strong. Lela, you have been very special to Ana, ever since she was born. It will give us joy to visit you in the valley, and we hope it will bring joy for you to visit us here." Ana liked the idea that she could bring joy to her family.

Clip clip. There was the bump of a braid on the plate beside Ana. She wanted to cover her head, but she felt *Tia* Lela's sleeve against her back.

Tia Lela said, "On this day, Ana, I give to you a cow."

A cow! Was it true? Ana loved rich warm milk, and it had been a long time since her family had had a cow. "Where is the cow?" she asked.

"We put her in your corral," said *Tia* Lela, just as the cow's head poked into the courtyard window.

Ana'a mother leaned toward Ana. "Every day, you and I will milk your cow together. How is that?"

"Yes, Mama. Yes!"

Ana's *abuela* moved close. Ana was not afraid when her grandmother held the scissors. Clip clip. Her *abuela* gave Ana a woven bag with long red tassels. "Now that you spin such fine yarn, Ana, you are ready to weave. When would you like to start?"

The First Hair Cutting

Ana could hardly believe the good words. Weave with her *abuela*! "Tomorrow!"

Ana pressed her *abuela*'s bag to her cheek to feel the soft alpaca yarn. She ran her fingers over the first design she wanted to learn. Weaving would be hard, but if Fidelia could learn, Ana could too.

Clip clip. It was her sister, Fidelia. "Ana," she said, "Papa says that on weekends and some days after school you can come to the mountains with me when I need help with the llamas. We can herd together again!" Ana could not ask for more.

Ana's younger brother stepped close. Clip clip. "I'm giving you this pebble that looks like a little bird." Ana touched the smooth pebble. It would bring her luck.

Clip clip. Clip clip. Little hands and big hands touched Ana's braids. Then braids dropped onto the plate and beside them notes and coins, more presents, even treats.

When the clipping stopped, Ana touched her head. There were no more braids. Her hair felt like new stubby plants when they first grew in the fields. Her mother smoothed the little stubs of Ana's braids and fastened each stub with a colorful barrette.

Ana placed some of her presents on a *manta* and stuffed the rest into her new red bag. "*Tia* Lela, may we see the cow now?"

In the corral Ana's cow waited, dressed in a red *poncho*. Ana grasped her cow's tail. "Come on, cow. Dance with me now!"

Out of the corral they danced. The musicians played their flutes and drum. Ana swung her new red bag, and the tassels flew. Beside Fidelia and her brothers, beside Mama, Papa, her *abuela*, *Tia* Lela, her aunts, uncles, and cousins, with her cow, Ana danced and she danced.

The First Hair Cutting

Shepherds in the Mountains

Now that Tika was six years old, it was her turn to care for the family's twenty-five sheep. Every day, all day, she would be part of the group of eight children responsible for taking care of a herd of 180 sheep. In their village, this was a huge shepherding. Because grass nearby was grazed so low, shepherds climbed the nearby mountains to look for untouched grazing areas. Tika would be on her own with the sheep, far from home.

Tika had heard many mountain stories, told as fearsome adventures. Her older sister, Yolanda, was ending her time shepherding. She told Tika, "When you are with the sheep, you must keep your eyes open and your ears alert. Foxes live where you will be going." Yolanda also told Tika that she would accompany her sister until Tika could see what her days would be like and understand what she might do.

At sunrise on Tika's first day, the sisters walked through the early fog to collect the sheep in the family's corral. Tika was not much taller than the animals, but, like Yolanda, she clicked a little and begged a little. When the stragglers still refused to move, she tapped their legs with her slingshot.

Above the village, Tika and Yolanda met the herds of moving animals and the other young shepherds. For almost two hours, the shepherds ran straight up the steep paths to reach the wild grazing areas on Black Mountain. Tika held her breath when she stopped on the edge of a steep drop-off to look at the taller mountains nearby and the sacred snowcapped *Apus*, far away.

While the sheep grazed, the shepherds played. They shot stones with their slingshots and watched their missiles sail through the sky to land high up far away or low down in a valley. Some girls brought family weavings so they could roll them together and make hand-made dolls that they carried on their backs. Everyone danced and sang to the clear notes of the boys' flutes. "More, more," Tika pleaded. She loved to hear the clear notes fly like birds over high vast stretches.

Much of the time that they tended the sheep, Yolanda spun yarn. By watching, Tika saw how to pull and twist her own fluffs of sheep's wool. Side by side they also wove together, practicing the village patterns. When a lamb fell into a prickly bush, both girls untangled and pulled the little one out, feet first.

At the end of the day, with the other young shepherds, Tika and Yolanda performed their *raki raki*. The village sheep had mingled during the day, grazing and moving on, often as one large group. As the sunlight faded, all the sheep had to be separated and returned to their individual family corrals. Tika loved *raki raki* because it was also a weaving pattern that means "that which should be together is apart." Tika had watched her mother's hands bring selected yarns on top of the weaving only to make the yarns disappear on the back, join again on top, then separate. The *raki raki* pattern would not be easy, but it was an important pattern she hoped to learn some day.

After several days of shepherding together, Yolanda said, "Tika, Mama says this has to be our last day together. She needs me at home." Yolanda dressed a lamb with a small *manta* and tied a bell around its neck. She looked into its eyes. "Good bye, little lamb." She hugged her sister. "Tika, I will miss you. But everything is going well. You will know how to handle anything that comes up."

On her own the next morning, Tika at first rejoiced to feel free, alone, and in charge of everything in her life. She ran with the sheep and climbed up on big stones. Soon though, when other shepherds were not near, she missed Yolanda. She named her sheep. The curious one that made Yolanda laugh but made Tika angry, she named "Lunch Robber." Another she named *Huaylaka*, "Wayward Mother" because

Shepherds in the Mountains

she neglected her babies. She honored the easiest sheep with the names Hilario and Cristóbal, distinguished saints.

The young shepherds pushed sticks into the earth to tell the time of day. On her first day alone, Tika was glad when the stick cast no shadow. Full noon. She went right to the lunch she had hidden in her *manta*.

But one cloudy day, the sticks were useless. Fog drifted from distant mountains and rose up from the valleys. Tika could hardly see. Thicker clouds moved from above, swirling in black streaks. Soon it felt like night. Thunder sounded behind the mountains, and the shepherds knew lightning would soon follow. Then came rain, a sudden whirling from all directions.

One of the other shepherds shouted, "Here's a cave!"

"Caves are entrances to the underworld," parents told their children. "Never go into a cave." However Tika, long curious and wanting to avoid rain and hail, knew that the cave nearby might prove their only escape from the violent storm, even at the risk of meeting fearful spirits who might grab and carry one of them off.

All the shepherds raced for the cave opening, dragging in sheep and huddling together. In the darkness, Tika touched the cave wall and shuddered. She imagined that the opening must go on and on, deep into the mountain. She was glad to be crowded in a big group, even with sheep, bumping and baaing, their powerful smell of lanolin and wet wool. The lightning flashed closer. The thunder crash seemed to shake the cave's sides.

Frightened as they were, no one received a visit from the underworld—no ghost of an Inca soldier, no royal relay messenger, no distinguished mummy carried on a litter. Tika saw only a small charred bundle that some live person had burned as a payment of thanks to *Pacha Mama*, Mother Earth. It was believed that *Pacha Mama* could only receive messages by way of smoke, and it felt comforting to know that the Great Mother, already attracted here, would likely protect them all.

When the rain stopped, clouds rose into a bright mist, backed by the sun. Tika shivered in her wet clothes. However, she and the other shepherds stayed on the mountain, guessing it was still early. But real darkness came fast. No one owned a light to show the way home. Tika's thin-sandaled feet had to feel the edges of the paths.

Tika wondered about her parents. She knew that they were usually too busy with work to spend time worrying. When she or other family members were away, it was as-sumed that they were safe. Her parents knew that Tika would be close to *Pacha Mama*, to whom they left regular payments of appreciation.

Tika sensed it was very late. She should be home by now. Would her family fear something bad had happened? How glad she was to hear the dogs and her family looking for her. They met on the path. Her father asked, "Tika, are you all right? Where were you? What were you doing?"

Tika answered, "A big storm came. We didn't know to start home." To herself, Tika begged *Pacha Mama* that there would never again be a day as hard as that one.

But there were other hard days. Later in the season, one of the shepherds told Tika to watch her sheep with special care because many were pregnant. Tika wished Yolanda could be at her side. She had only once seen a sheep give birth. She knew little of what lay ahead.

Soon, one lamb or more were born each day. At the first birth, Tika feared that the blood would never stop coming. The baby lamb seemed healthy, and in a few minutes it walked on its own scrawny legs. In contrast, the mother looked frighteningly weak. Tika had heard that sheep in such a condition must immediately feast on extra good grass, so she led the new mother to graze and was relieved to see some strength come back. By night they were able to make the journey down the mountain.

New babies kept coming. One day Tika found herself with three mothers and their three newborns. The mothers would be ready, but how could they all travel the long way home? Tika wished she could ask for help, but the other young shepherds were busy with their new lambs. She decided to carry two lambs in her *manta* and the other in her arms. She struggled downhill, keeping the lambs close. When she felt almost hopeless, she heard her mother and Yolanda on the path.

"Here I am. Look!" Tika called. They were overjoyed to gather the three new lambs into their arms.

Not many days afterward, Tika was sitting against a rock practicing her weaving when she heard cries. She quickly rounded up her sheep. Her favorite lamb was missing.

Another shepherd ran down the slope to look. Tika heard his shouts. A fox had grabbed the lamb. Tika stood above and picked up a stone as heavy as she could lift. Could she scare the fox without hurting the lamb? She tossed the stone. When it landed, the fox jumped and, in the noise and confusion, dropped the lamb. Tika scrambled down the slope and found the baby lying in the grass. She cried with relief to see that it was still alive. She wiped off the blood and soothed the lamb that had been born so recently, under her watch.

At home Tika's mother was excited to hear about her daughter's rescue of the precious lamb. "We knew you would discover what to do if bad things happened, Tika," she said. "Now you are familiar with the mountains. You know what can happen. You know the animals. And you have done well as part of our family."

Despite other hard days in the mountains with the sheep, Tika remembered her shepherding year as one of the happiest of her life.

Shepherds in the Mountains

THE
Ice Mountain

Voices were hushed in the house of Tomas. Visitors came and went, and his wife stayed near, watching for a sign of change. Across the courtyard, voices were also hushed in the house of his son, Alberto. The injured man's eight-year-old grandson, Juan, wondered whether he would ever play ball with Grandpa again or hear Grandpa's nighttime stories. Since the terrible mishap, no one had been able to sleep.

Earlier in the week, on their way home from the fields, Grandpa Tomas and his ox were startled when a bus tried to pass them on the narrow rutted road. With his horn, the ox rammed Tomas in the side and pushed him against a wall. At first friends feared Tomas was dead. But at home his eyes flicked open, and his wife tended him well.

The *curandero* made extra visits to the village, but no ritual or tincture had yet been strong enough for a cure. The only hope, concluded Alberto, was to make a direct appeal to a powerful mountain god, a distant *Apu* said to care for the health of people. Alberto and Juan would travel to the yearly ceremony of the *Qoyllu Riti, Star of the Snow*. They would each attend as the spirit of a bear, an *ukuku*, thought to have rare abilities.

Besides wearing the symbolic bear costume—layers of black braided yarns, white knitted face mask pulled over the head, and on top a huge puff of real fur that stood for Bear— what must a bear do, the boy wanted to know. "Be strong. Lead acts of excitement, yet keep order—like a herder urging the llamas to roam while keeping them together to stay and graze." Juan could not imagine such a task.

Juan had only a few days to learn the dance steps of the *ukuku* bears. He had to learn them well because on the pilgrimage the bear's rigorous steps, every part of his body in constant motion, would save him from freezing on the mountain.

Although Juan was proud of his elevated role, his first pilgrimage to the great ceremony on the ice mountain, he was distressed when he heard that there were two parts to the plan. The first night, Juan, his father, and his mother would run, dance, and climb for five hours with thousands of other pilgrims to reach an encampment just below the high mountain glacier. That

would begin three days of ceremonies near the Sanctuary of Jesus Christ, a remote church scarcely used except for the time of the pilgrimage.

The next night, in darkness, with a group of about fifty *ukukus*, his father would climb higher, onto the snowcap, and stay for four hours of ritual activities. Finally, his father and the others would each secure on his back a chunk of glacial ice. Back home, the power of that pure ice, melted to water, should cure Tomas. But last year, during this brave effort, someone from their own village had slipped and fallen to his death.

"Will you come back?" Juan asked.

Alberto hugged his son. "Of course. I will be very careful."

On a clear day, a truck awaited the village pilgrims. The musicians climbed up, and then the dancers dressed in costume holding their masks and waving goodbye. Juan's mother, a woman much admired in the village for her fine and energetic dancing, stepped in next along with a few other women, all dressed in their layers of hand-bordered skirts and finest weavings.

The truck pulled away. The sunshine glittered off elaborate portable shrines and crosses. Gigantic decorative candles stood as tall as some travelers. The pilgrims sang in high-pitched voices while the music of drums, horns, and flutes rose in a cloud of sound.

After the numbing night on the cold open truck, the travelers jumped out and sang with joy at the sight of the snow-capped

The Ice Mountain

peaks. Juan's thoughts were fixed on the white glaciers that touched the sky. His father would venture up there? Despite his worried thoughts, Juan was excited to start the five hours of climbing, dancing, and running with the other pilgrims to reach the high encampment.

Already newcomers danced their individual and separate steps below the blinding white mountains. Some, meant to impersonate the *Qolla* people of the eastern Inca kingdom, slapped the ground with their whips and hand-braided slingshots. *Chunchus*, wearing headdresses and carrying palm spears to suggest jungle people, chased each other to provoke mock battles. A *Machula*—parody of a city business man in a long black tail coat, top hat, and huge-nose mask—tried to grab a young *Qolla* dancer's whip; the young one, in turn, grabbed the man's cane. The road filled with unfamiliar people dressed in costumes Juan had

never seen before. In high spirits, many moved straight up the mountain. Donkeys mixed in, loaded with bundles of kindling.

From all directions voices rose, singing in high staccato. Juan wanted to cover his ears against the discord of different tunes sung all at the same time—competing songs of love, longing, sadness, celebration, fertility, and the beloved verses of "Little Vicuña." The clash seemed intended to overpower everything familiar.

Juan's grandfather once tried to tell him about the puzzling activities of *Qoyllu Riti*, the pilgrimage where people seemed to be turning the usual activity of life around, upside down and downside up. Grandpa had talked about the clashes of two forces. "Juan, don't forget *hanan* and *hurin*—up and down. There are two opposite parts of everything. Even two strange opposites can remain together like our old traditions and our love of Jesus Christ."

What Juan remembered made little sense to him. With sadness and longing he wished he had listened to everything his grandfather had told him on those dark nights when he was sitting on Grandpa's lap or in a bed nearby. Now Juan was full of questions about these days on the mountain. Would he ever talk with his grandfather again?

Someone set up an elaborate altar brought from the village, and when others moved aside Juan knelt on the frozen earth. He whispered, "Jesus Christ and Great *Apu* above us, can you hear me? I beg you to send my father back with no harm. I beg you to save Grandfather. And please, I do not want to freeze here. So please save me too." He soon felt others crowding next to him so he ran off.

As cold as it sometimes felt back in the village, on the mountain in June, the beginning of the cold dry season, Juan could not stop shaking. He felt frozen in place. His father saw him. "Juan,

keep dancing your steps. Never
stand still. Move like this to make
your body warm." They danced
together in wild unrestrained turns
while Papa called out, "Leap,
Juan, leap. Dance, Juan, dance."

As they pushed up the steep
mountainside, Juan's father sang
high and loud. In his *ukuku* bear
role as exciting entertainer, he
whistled into the small bottle that
hung around his neck. People
turned to watch as he chased
Juan's mother, trying to hand her
his enormous bundle.

"You cannot trick me, Bear!"
she loudly protested. "You, who are strong and powerful, ask a
heavy-burdened woman to also carry your bundle?"

Juan's father, begging and pleading, found space to
kneel beside her. "I am really an old man, dressed like a bear!
Help me, lovely señora."

"You are no old man!" Laughing she bumped into Juan
and fell back where someone in the crowd caught and held
her. Everyone shouted with delight.

Juan tried to stay near his father. But after the first three
hours of running, climbing over rocks, and dancing up the
mountain with everyone, it was hard to keep up. Two more
hours before Juan could stop. Despite his strong Andean lungs,
he gasped for breath in the thin and frigid mountain air.

Juan saw his father higher up waiting for him. "Juan, keep
up your spirit. This cold is our hardship. To suffer for these three
short days heals us all. Think of the two opposites to everything
in life: if you know deep cold, you will know deep warmth."

Juan passed young women nearby, their hands holding woven cloths in which they would present offerings of thanks to *Pacha Mama* and The Lord of the Mountain. And from the sky a condor swooped down.

"Look," people called out, for the condor is considered the messenger of a mountain *Apu*. But the condor passed and flew into the valley far below.

By the time the mountain spread its shadow on the ever-moving pilgrims, Juan's family reached the high encampment. Everyone seemed in a joyous mood, holding out cups for *chicha* beer.

Like the other pilgrims around them, Juan's family set up a makeshift plastic tent. The smell of roasting food and the rising smoke surrounded them in their tent. Mama filled and refilled three white enamel cups with hot stew, but Juan could only wonder whether the skimpy covering above could keep their blood from freezing that night. Soon they wrapped themselves in their weavings and lay close. Juan faded into cold almost-sleep.

In the early morning, crystals of deep frost had formed on the ground. Juan crawled out and faced a crowd. This morning, he liked the feel of other bodies bumping against his, the warm damp breath, a small vapor that formed like a web around them.

Sellers had set up a small market with miniature objects for pilgrims to buy and leave, to remind the Mountain God of their pleas. Serious men talked of their dreams to own a minivan. Juan dared to kneel and play with a small red truck. Then he remembered that his family had a more desperate wish.

When Juan stood, he faced a very old man. He could hardly see the wrinkled face behind the heavy pile of *ponchos*.

"*Ukuku*, young bear," the old man said. "I want to talk with you."

Juan led him to their tent shelter where they sat on two of his mother's beautiful rolled-up skirts and huddled in her woven wool and alpaca *mantas*. With great interest the old man's aged fingers traced bands of patterns on a weaving. He showed Juan. "You know this pattern, *cuti* means *that which turns around*. Put *cuti* together with *pacha*, earth, and you have *pachacuti*, the turning around and upside down of everything on earth."

Juan was curious to hear more, and the man said, "These lovely *mantas* and their patterns let me know where you come from. I have been to your village many times. I know your grandfather." He brightened and touched Juan's face. "You look like him. Young bear, you must be confused by this chaos around us. But your grandfather would know what I know. I wonder what he has told you."

His grandfather! Momentarily Juan choked up, but the man continued. "Do you know of the Pleiades, the star group that the ancestors thought to be their celestial life-giving mother? For two months of the year, those stars leave the sky and travel to the underworld.

People used to fear a terrible disaster when they lacked protection from the Pleiades," the old man continued. "Infertility, poor crops, sick herds, human sickness, accidents, sudden death—a small or large turn-around of peoples' lives. They feared not a good but a bad *pachacuti*." The old man continued, "We have come here to enact disorder and upheaval. Maybe we will scare away what we fear. But do not worry, son. The Pleiades are about to return. They are associated with the rising of the sun. They will bring relief."

The old man closed his eyes and seemed to fall asleep but mumbled softly. Juan felt some relief as small parts of the past and present began to come together. But the dim light outside reminded him that his father would soon leave for his terrible climb.

He was glad when his father crawled into the tent to get him and hand him a candle. Outside the family pushed through the crowd and waited to enter the Sanctuary of Jesus Christ, the honored church on the steep slope.

A clanking of metal signaled the opening of the churchyard gate. Some pilgrims continued dancing outside. His father and mother each lit a candle and prayed for Grandpa Tomas. But in the presence of sacred relics and Jesus on the cross, all gleaming in candlelight, Juan could only make a short desperate plea for his grandfather and steady himself enough to bow his head.

Outside, above them, the glaciers shimmered in white moonlight. Juan wrapped his arms around his bear being. Looking high in the sky, he imagined himself climbing the ridges on the glacier where his father would soon set forth. The air smelled of the crisp crackling cold.

The *ukuku* bears prepared to ascend. Juan's father had to leave. "By morning," he told Juan, "you will see us all return." He put his arm around Juan's shoulder. Juan held tightly as if his bear

The Ice Mountain

strength could prevent his father from stepping away. But he heard his mother call, "Alberto!" Soon she and the other wives walked with their husbands to the edge of the glacier to say long private goodbyes.

Carrying their flickering lights, the *ukuku* bears stretched out ropes and moved slowly, helping each other up the high narrow rim along the edge of the glacier. Against the white and enormous sky, his father and others seemed as fragile as the smallest of creatures. Juan and his mother watched until the climbers' lights were over-powered by stars. The dark figures disappeared behind the glacier's edge.

In his mind Juan could see his father. No tracks to guide him. The empty white space. Caution before each step. Snow or ice? He murmured, "Papa, where are you? Jesus Christ and Father *Apu*, spare Papa. Bring him down." But what could Juan do? His father was testing himself against the great Mountain.

A somber feeling spread, even as women poured homemade *chicha* beer into peoples' cups and passed around the welcome drink. In front of another portable shrine, Juan

The Ice Mountain

and his mother knelt until Juan leaned on his mother's shoulder, almost asleep.

"Juan," she said, "It is hard to wait but it is part of being here. We learn to wait, to discover patience. Your father will come back by morning. Go have a short rest. I will wake you if you are needed."

Alone Juan lay down under the skimpy plastic and shut his eyes in the empty cold darkness. He curled up, like a dog. He thought of his father's heavy steps. Was he sinking? Was he covered with snow? Maybe he had lost a glove. What if his feet froze? Could he still breathe through the mask that covered his head and face? He knew that his father, with the others, would stay through the late night, spending the traditional time together to talk and sing.

Juan pulled his mother's soft *manta* close. He fell into a dazed sleep. He could not help but think that he himself would freeze to death, right here, right now.

When he pushed back the edge of the tent cover, Juan looked into the darkness, transfixed by the stars' brilliance. He had never felt the Milky Way so close, like a true river in the sky.

Leaving the tent, Juan searched for his mother. At last he found her near the image of Jesus Christ painted on a famous rock. They looked for a good place to wait for the bears' return. Someone, looking at the sky, said, "The Pleiades have returned! Look. You can see six of the seven stars, right there." At the same time tiny lights moved back down the glistening mountain. There was an outcry of joy.

The brave *ukuku* bears descended placing each footstep carefully. And there was Juan's father, ice burden tied to his back.

Finally, standing on the firm earth, Papa and the others let their burdens down.

They all knelt, talking to the Mountain. Papa said, "I here express my gratitude, great *Apu*, to be safe, to be alive at this holy place. Allow me to remove the sacred ice to my village. I beg that Juan's beloved grandpa will drink and be healed."

Papa said to Juan and his wife, "At this moment I feel cold in my hands and feet, but warmth is spreading in the rest of my body. I sense that the Lord of the Mountain has heard our entreaties, and I beg that my own dear father is already recovering."

The Ice Mountain

Juan asked, "Papa, what was it like? Was it slippery? Did anyone fall?"

"For now, dear Juan, it is hard for me to talk. But everyone is all right." He suddenly smiled, lifted the glacial ice, and handed it to Juan. The boy's knees almost collapsed. He nearly fell forward from the weight before he pushed the cold chunk back into his father's waiting arms.

The moon stretched light in the sky as if to herd the great number of subdued pilgrims who quietly danced down-slope, then danced in place to the bands who played peacefully together. The pilgrims knelt as they waited for the sun to rise. As the sun's first color showed, everyone on the mountain prayed in silence. His mother and others cried. Some, like their Inca ancestors, blew kisses. It was time for Juan and his parents to leave. They danced and ran down to the village truck.

Once in the truck, Juan's parents arranged protective weavings around the precious ice. On the way home, everyone in the truck marveled that the Pleiades had returned to the sky. Juan was glad to have time with his father, glad to finally share what he had learned from the old man. As they talked, Juan and his father agreed that their customs were part of their lives and who they were. The customs made them whole, brought them together, taught them, healed them, and gave them hope.

The truck finally stopped outside their village. Everyone rushed to welcome the brave pilgrims, anxious to see and stroke the ice from the mountain glacier.

Alberto carried the bundle to Tomas, who still lay in bed but twisted with a wince to sit up and hug his son and grandson.

Juan's father melted the glacial ice into water, and Tomas drank from the bottle.

"I have something for you," Grandpa told Juan. He reached under his bed, found the soccer ball that Juan had rolled there for safekeeping before he left, and, with a large grin, weakly rolled it to the boy.

Grandpa Tomas took Juan's mother's hand and looked at his son and grandson. "I am feeling better. Surely everything you have all done, your prayers and pilgrimage too, must have made this happen. Thank you, my dear bears."

Juan kissed Grandpa's cheek.

The sacred pilgrimage of Qoyllu Riti continues to this day, but in recent decades the ritual of climbing the heights to bring down healing ice is no longer practiced because of the rapid melting and loss of Andean glaciers.

The Ice Mountain

Tell Me,
Bright Stars

After conquering the Inca people more than 500 years ago, the Spanish invaders forced all indigenous people to become Catholic. Today, many Inca descendants continue their traditional beliefs but still consider themselves Catholic, in their own way, merging Christian and Inca holidays.

Above her village, high in the Andes Mountains, Rosa led her llamas back for the night. In two days it would be Christmas. But this year Rosa hardly cared. She passed visitors wandering through the ruins of the old temples and palaces of her Inca ancestors. Other strangers stepped out of a red bus.

Such excitement. "*Bella, bella*," she heard. "How beautiful!"

Rosa did not want to hear strangers talk about her beautiful village. Last week, hail pounded the ground, ruining the early potatoes. Her family was already short of food, and, with Mama about to have a baby, they needed potatoes to pay Mama's midwife, *Doña* Cecelia.

Damp and shivery. That's how the kitchen felt these days without the usual smells of Mama's hot soups and stews. Rosa and her family sat down to hard-boiled eggs and soup as thin as tea. Rosa felt as empty as a sky without stars.

Rosa's brothers, Tomas and Roberto, talked softly. "Mama counted the potatoes. There is no way there will be enough."

Her little sister, Maria, looked at Rosa. What can I tell her? Rosa thought. Will we have to choose between the midwife for Mama and food to eat?

After dinner, Rosa and Mama unrolled their looms and wove together. Rosa loved this time together, Mama finishing the new baby shawl and Rosa practicing the designs of her village, making *jakimas*, long narrow ribbons of weaving.

"Mama, look." Rosa held up twelve *jakimas*. Half were her favorite design: *chaska*, which means "star."

"Rosa," Mama said, "maybe your little stars will bring us luck."

When Mama rolled up her weaving early, Rosa remembered that her mother was tired like this just before

Maria was born. How Rosa wished the baby had come, that *Doña* Cecilia had helped, that Mama was fine, and that everyone's worries were over.

Rosa stood by the window. "Tell me, bright stars. What can I do?"

On the day before Christmas, Rosa begged Papa to go to the holiday market in the city of Cusco.

"We will all go," Papa said. Rosa felt secretly sure that one of them could find something to give to the midwife, something even better than potatoes.

There were huge baskets and tiny baskets, felt hats with colored ribbons, and even a few fresh-smelling pine branches. Sellers laid out tangerines, bananas, and paper cones of popped corn.

When no one was looking, Tomas, Rosa, Roberto, and Maria dropped beneath the rickety tables. They crawled beside the feet of people and animals and ran their hands over the ground.

Tomas discovered two pine cones. Roberto picked up a smashed fig. Rosa watched him breathe in its rich sweetness, then put it in his pocket. Maybe he would take it to Mama. But that would not help. Maria found the wing and head of a broken angel.

"Would *Doña* take this for helping Mama?" Maria asked.

"No," said Rosa. "We need something better."

Rosa crawled under the next table. Nothing.

They heard Papa, "Come, *niños*. Let's go."

As they headed home, Rosa saw the red bus. How many times it came these days! Suddenly the windows opened and strangers called out, "¡*Feliz Navidad*!" Out flew handfuls of candies.

"¡*Feliz Navidad*!" the children called back and scrambled to find the treats.

Tell Me, Bright Stars

"Would *Doña* take these?" Rosa asked Roberto.

"No. Not candies," he said. So Rosa unwrapped one candy and saved a few more for herself. The rest she would take to Mama.

Mama leaned against the wall near the cook-fire.

"We brought you treats," Rosa called.

Mama hugged her and the others. "My present for you is here. Feel the little kicks. This baby wants to come see us."

"Is the baby coming now?" Rosa asked.

"Maybe soon," Mama said.

The taste of Rosa's last sweet candies made her think of the friendly visitors. Then she had an idea. She grabbed her weavings and ran. Shadows spread across the village. The air smelled of smoke from dying cook fires. Soon the sun would go behind the mountains. But Rosa ran up, up, up. In the distance, there was the red tour bus. Rosa nearly bumped into a visitor. The woman smiled. Rosa held up her weavings.

The woman looked carefully at each one, especially at the *chaska* weavings. "What is this *diseño*?" she asked. Rosa pointed above the mountains to the most glittering star. "*Chaska.*"

For a moment the woman looked up. "*Chaska* must mean star? Inca stars on Christmas Eve!"

Rosa nodded. She wants to buy, Rosa thought, and held the weavings closer to the woman. Other visitors turned the bend. When they saw what Rosa had brought, everyone seemed excited, "How much?"

Before she knew what was happening, coins and bills fell into Rosa's hands. No one even made her bargain.

When the strangers left, they called, "¡*Bella bella, Feliz Navidad*!" Rosa ran downhill, the cool coins and paper money tight in her hands.

She pulled open the courtyard door. "Mama, Papa!"

The light of the oil lamp showed Mama in bed, Papa and the midwife, *Doña* Cecelia, beside her. On the floor her sister and brothers huddled in their blankets.

Rosa dropped the coins and bills on the bed. She told her story.

Papa said, "*Doña* Cecelia. We do have something to trade. Look what our Rosa brought!"

Rosa stared at the surprised faces. She could hardly believe her weavings could bring such happiness.

"*Una niña*. A girl!"

Lumpy blankets rolled and bumped. Out came all the children.

Mama said, "Each of you, come hold your little sister."

When it was Rosa's turn, she snuggled the warm baby close and stared into her eyes. Rosa's fingers searched for the one *chaska* weaving she had hidden in her hat.

"I saved this for you." She waved the *chaska* weaving back and forth. The baby gurgled. "Welcome, little sister. *Feliz Navidad*."

They named the baby Chaska.

Tell Me, Bright Stars

TO
Weave the Milky Way

On the high slopes of the Andes mountains of Peru, Casiana and her young friends practiced the weaving patterns of their village. When they took their family sheep to graze, they set up handmade looms and wove. They wove beside streams. They wove in the shadows of old Inca walls. They wove on sunny days and on days when it rained so hard that everyone raced to find cover beneath high overhangs of rock.

To Weave the Milky Way

The children learned their village patterns by weaving *jakimas*, long narrow bands of weaving that everyone used for braids, for tying on hats, for belts, for the whole family to hang jugs on the wall. Sometimes the children traded *jakimas*. Sometimes they gave a special *jakima* as a present to a friend. Young weavers wanted to make larger pieces some day. They would need to know and combine many patterns: *punta, tanka churu, quesua, ñawi, mayu kuti*. Generations of weavers had passed down to them more than forty different village patterns.

One Sunday, market day, in the courtyard of their house, Casiana sat beside her older brother Ramon, watching him weave a belt he said he wanted to sell. He was combining the patterns he knew, and on both edges, he wove Casiana's favorite, *mayu kuti,* the Milky Way. It was Casiana's dream to weave *mayu kuti*. She liked its two meanings, *the Milky Way with its river of stars* and *the sacred river with islands*. In the Inca way of thinking, the sky mirrors the land, the land the sky. Water circulates through the lakes, rivers, streams, and oceans and through the sky where the whole world is held in sacred water.

Casiana had learned two patterns. Now she wanted to weave the pattern that said so much. But for her, learning came with mistakes and turnarounds, tangles and twists. It seemed that no one else had to pull out so many threads. Recently, she had even stayed away from her friends so they could not see her struggles. She knew that she should not try to hide. Everyday life was supposed to include every one. But what could she do?

"How I wish I could weave like you," she told her brother.

Ramon smiled. "When you are ready, you will find your way. I know you."

"You do *not* know me. I *am* ready," said Casiana.

Many times Ramon had told her to watch his hands. He

must have thought he could help her learn. But it had never worked. Ramon smiled at the frown on her face.

"Why are you looking at me?" she asked.

"You surprise me," he told her.

Casiana thought, "Ramon is my brother. He knows I am not just someone who cannot do things right. I am a fast runner. I play soccer with everyone. He likes the stones I find that look like little animals. But can he ever understand?"

Later, at the village market, her family laid out old and new weavings to sell. They sat next to others with pottery figurines, small bird whistles, painted beads, earrings—things that outsiders might want to buy and villagers could not get by trading potatoes. Casiana's mother and *abuela* wove their wide *mantas*. Ramon worked to finish his belt. Casiana needed a new backstrap loom for a new weaving so she made a short new loom to learn *mayu kuti*. She started by counting and stretching out long lengths of yarn, alternating two colors. This was the tradtional Andean weaving way: even a narrow warp was set with the warp yarns so close that the back-and-forth weft yarns hardly showed.

Casiana was glad to be here, part of three generations of family weavers, at work side by side. The elders created elaborate compositions. Patterns mixed and mirrored, next to each other, interlocked, or upside down. When she touched the *mayu kuti* in Mama's weavings, she knew she was touching stars.

A stranger walked by and watched Ramon remove the pieces of loom to free his finished belt. The woman said she wanted to buy. She made him an offer. Ramon, still admiring his own good work, said, "No" without looking up. Casiana poked him with her toe until he named a price he would take to give up one of his first belts. To his surprise, the woman paid him just what he wanted.

"Thanks, sister," Ramon called back to Casiana as he ran to tell his friends.

"How I wish I were like Ramon," Casiana thought. She was glad he had sold his weaving. She picked up the remains of his loom to wrap in a cloth and take home for him.

Back in their courtyard, Casiana again tried to weave, this time on the new little loom, but in no time the same old words came back. "So many threads to pick up. So many places to make mistakes. Wrong again." She untied her narrow loom and dropped it on the dirt floor. "*Mayu kuti* is too hard for me."

Her mother put her arm around Casiana's shoulders and seemed to talk into the air. "A woman from North America asked why we do not put the great amount we know on paper, to help teach you children patterns. But how would it help if a daughter could not learn by watching her mother or by letting someone guide her hands—or by just seeing everyone trying again and again? Watching takes patience, and Casiana, you have that."

That night Casiana ran out to the corral to stand under the Milky Way. There she felt part of the brilliant world around her, drawn into the power of light, the river of stars overhead. She looked for the constellations like the Black Llama and Black Baby Llama that she, like other Inca people, saw as the negative black shapes between stars.

Her *abuela* came to stand at Casiana's side. She stroked her grandaughter's soft hair. "Did you know that

maya kuti is my favorite pattern too?" Casiana hugged her *abuela*, they talked, and soon said goodnight.

It took time to fall asleep; starlight came through evey small window. Casiana felt the light transforming her whole village. When sleep came, in her dreams Casiana hitched her loom to the crescent moon and traveled through the night sky. On her mother's woven blanket, she floated over the river of stars and through the Milky Way. She was weaving the curving line, and inside each curve, the circles of stars appeared.

In the morning, Casiana knew what she must do. She ate her breakfast of warm quinoa porridge. In a cloth she

To Weave the Milky Way

wrapped her lunch—a hunk of cheese, two hard-boiled eggs, a small piece of a hot pepper, one boiled potato, and popped corn. Glad that her father had the llamas with him, Casiana gathered the sheep.

"Mama, today I *will* weave *mayu kuti*," she said as she started to leave.

"I know you will. And take these balls of yarn. I spun them for you. My determined girl, you may weave the *mayu kuti* and even want to make a new loom."

Her *abuela* said, "Casiana, take my new *manta* to carry your things today."

As Ramon left for school, he tied a narrow *jakima* ribbon around the dog. "Good luck," he called.

Off Casiana ran, bundle on her back, spindle under her arm, her dog jumping at her feet.

On the mountain side, where she stopped for the sheep to feed, Casiana saw her friends with their animals. Some had already started weaving. They waved. She called. What patterns were they trying today? But she did not really want to know.

Casiana was glad to have her sheep nearby. She bent and looked into the eye of her smallest lamb. Someday she would weave the pattern *ñawi*, the eye of an animal, *ñawi* that also means the eye of the potato—the spot where the seed is planted, the place from which *Pacha Mama* lets green sprouts grow.

To Weave the Milky Way

    Casiana sat on her *abuela's manta*, laid out her mother's balls of yarn, and unrolled her narrow loom. She tied one end around her back, the other around her big toe.

    Now that her yarns stretched like a bright road in front of her, she leaned back to pull them tight. Casiana could hardly wait. Here I go, *mayu kuti*.

    Her fingers seemed to know their way. She turned one of her sticks on end. With her fingers, she picked up yarn strands that made the first pattern line. She pulled through her weft. The next line and the next went well, too. But when she stopped to scratch her toe, her loom flipped over and hung loose upside down.

    Casiana got up to make things right, but as hard as she tried, the long warp yarns would not line up again. She lay back and looked at the mountain peaks against the pale sky. One pattern she had learned was *puntas*, "mountain points," tops of the mountains like those right above her. And she had learned *kinko*, "the curving way." Every day she climbed the *kinko* way, on the steep and curving paths that twisted around the mountains.

When Casiana got up again to straighten her threads and stretch her loom out straight, she found her favorite sheep too close. How could she hold her loom and make the sheep move? Then her feet kicked the balls of Mama's yarn. She

To Weave the Milky Way

struggled to catch them, but the more she chased yarn, the more the sheep pulled and played.

And then, her *abuela* walked up the path, bringing the piglets to graze. When she saw the wild tangle—Casiana, the sheep, the yarn—she started laughing. Finally, she stopped and sat down. "Casiana, my mother used to tell me, 'What is done is done. What is coming is coming.' You have good things coming."

"How can that be?"

Her *abuela* just stroked Casiana's hair.

When the other young shepherds saw Casiana's *abuela*, they came from all directions, running and carrying their looms, their animals following. Even Ramon came. He must have slipped out of school.

Her *abuela* unrolled her backstrap loom. She leaned forward, rocked back. Her fingers moved through sets of colors. Mid-line her *abuela* changed to a different technique that made her weaving look even richer. A pattern sometimes grew a little too long or a surprise slipped through her sure hands, but she kept on going.

With everyone there, Casiana straightened her own yarns. She whispered, "*Mayu kuti*, bright river of stars, if I can bring you here, I will always feel your light." Even by day, it was as if she could touch the bright stars in the Milky Way. The rhythm began as her fingers found their way through the threads. Her pattern began to grow.

But the first star in her Milky Way looked too small. A mistake? She stopped. Then, like her *abuela*, she just kept weaving.

Up to the next line she moved. And the next. And the next. Like climbing high stone steps, like climbing a ladder to the sky.

Her friends said, "Good for you, Casiana. You have got it right."

Ramon said, "Casiana, I knew you could do it."

Casiana's curving line grew as she counted.

Then, to her surprise, Casiana saw that her hands were full of stars.

To Weave the Milky Way

The Old Man, the Llamas, and Machu Picchu

Many years ago, in the mountains that rise high above the Urubamba River, an old man lived in a small stone house near his four sons. Their village was so distant and isolated that it received few visitors.

The old man liked to talk of a long-ago experience that still excited his mind daily. As a boy he had gone with his father to a cloud-covered mountain to help foreigners cut back thick growth and reveal finely cut stone walls that suggested the ruins of an entire Inca city. The old man's wife had loved to hear the stories of his adventures, which grew more elaborate at every telling. But she had died years ago, and by now no one would listen, except his youngest son and his four precious llamas.

The old man dearly wanted to talk to his other sons, but they were too busy planting and harvesting potatoes and grains on the terraces near their home. Or they occasionally traveled back and forth to the jungle to plant and harvest the produce that could not grow at their high altitude: corn, squash, peppers, bananas, oranges, figs, and coca plants whose leaves were needed for traditional offerings and for healing or providing strength.

Every day the old man led his four beloved llamas to graze above the village. Because he spent much of his time on the heights, the old man was happy that his youngest son, Kori, came with him, bringing the rest of the family's herd of llamas and alpacas.

Kori listened with interest to his father's stories of discovering great steps and buried terraces. But Kori was even more intrigued by the four special llamas whom his father treated like a second family.

The old man and the llamas hummed back and forth to each other. When the llamas grazed nearby, the old man spoke and they seemed to listen with interest. "You deserve to spend the rest of your lives at that place where the enchanted mountain rises from the jungle and is encircled by a sacred river. I will take you and leave all of you there, with an important mission."

The llamas seemed to hum in the Quechua language that Kori could understand, words that reflected the animals' curiosity about going to the place of their old man's dreams. When they weren't playing or chomping on tough *ichu* grass, the llamas sometimes stared at the old man. He stared at them. He tried to respect their independence but gently sang sacred songs close to their ears and looked into their beautiful eyes. When their faces came close to his face, they were sometimes mischievous and ran away. But they always returned and played nearby.

The Old Man, the Llamas, and Machu Picchu

The old man told Kori, "Before I die I am going to find again that place, which they called Machu Picchu. How I wish you could come with me."

"I will, Papa," the boy said with excitement. They talked about their hopes of finding lost sections of the old Inca road system and tried to predict how long their journey would be.

The old man announced to his other sons, "Before I die, I must find that place from my childhood. Kori will come too, and we will leave tomorrow. I have promised my llamas to take them to a new and enchanted home."

His three other sons looked alarmed.

"Papa, at your age how could you make such a journey through the dense growth where you will not even see where you are? You will never find such a place. You and Kori must stay at home where you belong, with us."

The old man said no more. He just returned his llamas to their corral. But when it grew late at night, he woke Kori. The two were loading the journey's necessities into bags on his llamas' backs when the oldest son came over from the house where he lived with his wife and children.

"Papa, what are you doing?"

The old man said nothing.

"I cannot let you go, Papa," said the oldest son. "Even with Kori, a boy who's never traveled to such places. We know you have powerful thoughts inside your head. But by now this place may be only a dream you once had." His oldest son helped his father unpack the provisions, and Kori left for bed.

The next day the old man went to the potato terraces and found his oldest son. He said, "I am disappointed that you doubt my past life. You have even begun to make me unsure. Now I must go and prove to myself that the place is real. Come with me, and we will find out together."

The oldest son leaned against his foot plow. He could not leave the crops, he said. "Dear Papa, you are an old man. Try to forget such ideas."

The old man said nothing, just kicked his way back to his house, using his walking stick.

Some days later, the old man could not resist talking to Kori. "My boy, in truth I am a sad man. I will not be happy until I find out whether the place of my dreams is real. Before I die, I must take these four fine llamas to live there for the rest of their lives and serve a special purpose."

The Old Man, the Llamas, and Machu Picchu

Kori knew how much the llamas meant to his father. Some nights the old man stayed high on the slope so he and they could all sleep under the moon and stars. More and more often, Kori joined them.

One night, as soon as it grew dark and the family slept, the old man again packed up, this time to set off on his journey with no one but his llamas.

Carrying his stick, he walked only a short way before the llamas started to hum and he saw a figure running behind him. He heard Kori's voice." Papa, I know where you are going. I am going with you."

Just then the old man's oldest son also came up the slope. The llamas hummed with great intensity. Some made other sounds of distress.

The oldest son said, "Papa, I know how much this mission means to you. Go with Kori and your llamas, and with my good wishes. But find the place and come right home. If not, after seven days we will all have to leave our work and come looking for you."

The old man and Kori decided to find their way by following the silver thread of the Urubamba River far below. The moon lit the night, and they could see for great distances. Finally they found a section of the old Inca road. After long hours, the old man grew tired. They stopped and wrapped themselves in their *ponchos* and slept where they felt high and safe. The llamas rested close by.

In the morning, from the mountain top, they could see in all directions, the sun shining on surrounding heights, the clouds below, a condor flying through receding darkness and morning light. Using the small hard pellets the llamas had dropped in a pile, the boy made a fire and roasted some corn.

The old man was hungry but before he ate, he formed the llamas in a circle around him. He stood in the middle,

humming with them. He told his son, "I like to consult with my wise friends."

The old man found a flat stone that looked like an altar. He instructed his son to take from a *manta* the sacred coca leaves he had brought and lay them on the small *unkuña* weaving made for offerings. The son did as he was told. Then, to make an offering that *Pacha Mama*, Mother Earth, could receive, the boy put some coals from the fire and other coca leaves into a bowl. As the leaves burned, the smoke rose and floated in the air.

"*Pacha Mama*," the old man said, "please let us know the way over your mysterious land, for we are going on an important mission."

The Old Man, the Llamas, and Machu Picchu

The old man said to Kori, "Listen. I hear a voice. 'It is time to find your way through my dense land. Go down and there you will find bromeliads, orchids, and butterflies. Then you will hear the river. Look carefully for a bridge.'"

They left behind the thin silver strand of the river they had followed as they walked. It became humid and hot as the old man and boy pushed their way down through high green growth. With the bromeliads, orchids, and butterflies, they also found thorns, nettles, and bugs that scratched or bit their arms and legs. The old man, his son, and the llamas all tried to find the revered river they had seen so often from a high distance.

Finally they heard the sound of water, soft at first, then loud enough for the llamas to startle and make resounding, concerned noises. By nightfall, they crossed a bridge over the Urubamba River and in darkness continued beside the tumbling river. The llamas expressed their loudest fears and looked around carefully until their apprehensions subsided.

"We slashed a zig-zag path that went up almost to the sky," said the old man. They all helped search but could only find their way up a long and twisting road. The old man's eyes felt strained, and the climb tired him greatly.

They reached an area where the road grew into a flat wide space. As if in a trance, the old man's steps led him through an open gate and above long deep curving terraces, all cleared of tangled plants, roots, and leaning trees.

With Kori and the llamas nearby, the old man looked up at the ruins of a whole glorious city, now uncovered. Not even clouds hid the majestic sights nearby, for it was a clear night, and the moon was a gracious guide. The old man turned and saw the river below, small and silver in the bright night. Never before had he felt dizzy near steep edges, but he could hardly keep his balance and leaned heavily on his familiar stick.

The old man remembered the stone steps, now also clear of creeping green tangles that had long ago caught in his sandals. He, Kori, and the llamas walked in and out of roofless rooms. The llamas left to explore. They stretched their heads through windows. They found intimate spaces. Despite their natural fear of new encounters, they seemed at ease and enlivened, as if they had found a new home.

The old man joyously ran his hands over the stones, now mostly exposed. Each had a different texture that made him think of the days he could touch his wife's variety of weavings, knit hats, and bags.

The Old Man, the Llamas, and Machu Picchu

"You saw all this when you were younger than I am!" Kori exclaimed. But the old man was wondering how people once carved and placed the stones, how the stones grew out of the mountain. Everywhere he felt the spirit of the *huacas*, sacred objects. The old man recognized a large thin stone that looked like a greatly oversized fish, undoubtedly a *huaca*. It was formally set on end so its edges would echo the sharp edges of the mountains behind. He appreciated the *huaca's* possible double honor to the vital spirit of water—water in the full ocean and water given by high inland mountains.

They walked in silence along a wide stone path beside high stone walls, then up the steps that rose a great distance from the bottom to the top of the once-great city. The steps were delicate and narrow, but the llamas were expert navigators of narrow uphill paths and moved with ease and seeming delight. Their bright ear tassels, once provided at a special ceremony, made them look distinguished high in the ancient royal spaces.

Under the full moon, the llamas happily grazed on the tender grass surrounding the many stones. By dawn, when they seemed especially content, the old man raised his arms and spoke to the mountain, Machu Picchu.

"I have come to present four of the finest of all llamas. They will live here as did the people and animals of the old kingdom. Their offering will be to keep the grass from growing back around the stones."

The llamas began to make loud terrified noises that the old man had only heard when they neck-wrestled to prove their dominance in the group. The old man went from the lead llama to the lowest member. He knelt, they raised their heads, and he looked into the eyes of each. "I cannot stay," he said. "You must not follow us. You will lead a life of deep peace here, not alone but together. You will establish and follow your own leader."

"We had better leave now," the old man said to Kori. Softly he spoke again to the llamas. "I will miss you greatly, dear friends. But I have long promised to let you live at this splendid place where you can stand among the tall mountains, roam within the passages, between stone walls, and through open doorways."

Gradually all four llamas found more delicious grass that they seemed to greatly enjoy. The old man said, "May you and your descendants stay here forever to honor this place."

The Old Man, the Llamas, and Machu Picchu

Glossary

Names and other words that might be unfamiliar.

Words are from the Quechua language unless marked (Span.) Spanish or (Eng.) English.

Apu
A respectful title for important mountains, meaning "holy father" or "holy mother" mountain.

Chaska
A star; also the name of a weaving pattern with the star motif.

Chicha
Andean beer made of fermented corn.

Chunchus
Indigenous forest tribes, or dancers dressed to impersonate them.

Cochineal
A natural red textile dye made from insects that grow on cacti.

Kuri Inti
Gold Sun, a rather excessive name for Señor Mouse in "To Live Like Humans!" because an Inca Emperor was considered a son of the Sun and gold reflected that sun.

Curandero
An indigenous healer or medicine person (Span.).

Cuti
A great change, a turning around; also the name of a weaving pattern.

Duality
Inca concept that all things have an alternate side (Eng.).

Hunan and Hurin
The up or down section of each town or city. Also represents duality.

Ichu
A rough grass (*stipa ichu*) that grows at high altitude, used as a building material and forage for llamas and alpacas.

Jakimas
Narrow woven strips made by children to practice the village patterns (pronounced *ha key mas*).

Kanta
Girl named for a many-colored Andean wild flower.

Kiko
Wildflower used to make yellow textile dye (in the aster family).

Machula
Ceremonial impersonation of exploiters who wear top hats.

Manta
A square or rectangular woven blanket or shawl, usually intricately woven, used as a garment or carrying cloth. Its designs and layout identify the home of the wearer.

Mayu Kuti
A river with islands, or the Milky Way with its stars; also the name of a weaving pattern.

Pablucha
Son of Bear.

Pacha
The earth.

Pacha Mama
Mother Earth.

Pachacuti
Inca concept: A time of disruption— literally, when the world turns around. Also the name of a great Inca emperor.

Pleiades
The constellation, thought to have protective power, visible in the sky except for the few months when life on earth could be frought with danger. (Eng.); Pléyades (Span.).

Poncho
A woven garment with a head slit, usually worn by men. (Span.).

Qoylu Riti
Star of the Snow, the sometimes life-threatening three-day pilgrimage and ceremony.

Raki Raki
That which should be together is separated, also a traditional weaving pattern.

Tia
Aunt (Span.).

Tika
A girl named Flower.

Ukuku
Father bear.

Vicuñas
Wild camelids, related to llamas, alpacas, and guanacos (Span.). Thought by Inca people to be children of the mountain gods.